MASTERS OF WORLD PAINTING

D0840307

Rembrandt

HARRY N. ABRAMS, INC., PUBLISHERS, NEW YORK

AURORA ART PUBLISHERS, LENINGRAD

COMPILED AND INTRODUCED BY XENIA YEGOROVA
DESIGNED BY VIACHESLAV BAKHTIN
TRANSLATED BY VLADIMIR TRAVLINSKY

Library of Congress Catalog Card Number: 79-55128
International Standard Book Number: 0-8109-2220-7

Copyright © 1981 by Aurora Art Publishers, Leningrad

Created by Aurora Art Publishers, Leningrad,
for joint publication of Aurora and Harry N. Abrams, Inc., New York

PRINTED AND BOUND IN THE USSR

The works of Rembrandt, the eminent Dutch painter of the seventeenth century, constitute an integral part of the spiritual heritage left to his fellow-countrymen and mankind at large. Two of the best collections of his works are to be found in the Soviet Union, one in the Hermitage in Leningrad, the other in the Pushkin Museum of Fine Arts in Moscow. The thirty canvases now in the Soviet Union enable us to trace the intricate course of his development as a painter, to appreciate the remarkable range of his interests and experiments and to fathom the singularity of his art. Such canvases as his *Danaë*, *Holy Family* and *The Return of the Prodigal Son* have long been classed with the most brilliant achievements in the realm of painting. The two museums also contain many drawings and a remarkable collection of etchings.

Rembrandt's heritage consists mostly of portraits and paintings on Biblical and mythological subjects (known in the seventeenth century as "histories"). While portraits outnumber his narrative canvases, Rembrandt personally regarded the latter as definitely the more important. The seventeenth century showed a preference both for tangible reality and wide generalization. Despite the flourishing of various genres, such as landscape and portraiture, depicting the surrounding scene, the men of the seventeenth century particularly valued the synthetic "history" genre, for it is precisely in "history" pictures that weighty moral and psychological problems were treated.

Rembrandt began to work independently in 1625, after he had returned to his native Leiden upon completing, in Amsterdam, a six months' apprenticeship under Pieter Lastman. One of his most interesting and characteristic canvases of that early period is *Christ Driving the Money-changers from the Temple* (1626, Pushkin Museum). The speckled, rather light coloring is borrowed from Lastman, the figure of Christ wielding a whip goes back to Dürer's etchings. The traders and money-changers tumble over one another, filling the foreshortened space. Men clamor as they try to escape, dodge the whip, and save their money and ware. Anatomical faults are visible, and the perspective lacks conviction. Patently the work of a beginner, the picture smolders with a feverish glow characteristic of Rembrandt's distinctive manner. In the years to come, Rembrandt showed himself a master in the depiction of "passions" which played so great a role in the

spiritual culture of the seventeenth century. His ideas of man's spiritual world and the aesthetic vistas revealed to him in painting ripened with surprising rapidity. Soon he began to produce works marked by a high professionalism, by an interest in man's intense spiritual life, and an understanding of the value of light and atmosphere in expressing emotion. In this manner, the artist evolved that fabric of problems and solutions in painting which we always associate with the name of Rembrandt.

During the late 1620s Rembrandt painted numerous half-length self-portraits, as well as portraits of two or three of his acquaintances, proceeding from mere studies of facial expressions toward a more profound character study. A good example of this is the portrait known as *The Old Warrior* (ca. 1630, Hermitage). The sitter used to pose for Rembrandt during his Leiden years and was even thought some decades earlier to be his father, though evidence of that was lacking. The painter's interest was stirred by the model's nervous, vacillating mood, though in the canvas from the Hermitage collection this trait is toned down and the old man assumes a nobler appearance. A play of chiaroscuro and flowing brushwork outlining the contour enlivens his otherwise unattractive face. The painter is absorbed in a wide range of black textures: the black silk of the garments up against the cold surface of burnished steel, and the intense black of the velvet against the glint of light on the ostrich feathers. The man's apparel is not in keeping with the prevailing style of the time, for Rembrandt had selected articles of clothing according to their artistic appeal and their associative value in lifting the portrayed from the humdrum of life onto a higher plane. The metal breastplate turns the picture into a portrait of a "warrior," while the feathered beret suggests the so-called Burgundy dress (a free imitation of sixteenth century fashions, favored on the stage and in "history" paintings; Rembrandt always used this apparel in later years, both in his "histories" and non-commissioned portraits).

From 1631 on Rembrandt began to produce portraits which were undoubtedly commissioned, one of the earliest of these being *Portrait of a Scholar* (1631, Hermitage). Whereas pictures of modest size painted on wood were characteristic of the preceding years, the *Scholar* is an imposing canvas whose composition is based on the combination of splashes of black, white, and gold. In this portrait the artist endeavored to reveal the momentary state of mind of his subject, something alien to the conventional type of official portraits: one sees the scholar bowed over his desk writing, when something suddenly distracts him, and he turns to look over his shoulder. This note of obvious animation accounts for the portrait's success. Other works similar to *Portrait of a Scholar* earned Rembrandt wide recognition and also, as a mark of respect and confidence, an order for a canvas to be known as *The Anatomy Lesson of Doctor Tulp* (1632, Mauritshuis, The Hague), a large group portrait of members of the Amsterdam Surgeons' Guild. It is thought that the completion of this canvas is responsible for Rembrandt's final move to Amsterdam.

During the period from 1632 to 1636 Rembrandt produced an exceptional number of commissioned portraits. Typical of these is *Portrait of a Young Man* (1634, Hermitage). The sitter's face wearing a somewhat vacant, though affable smile is rather trite, but, on the other hand, the features and bearing give an impression of unaffected ease without a trace of stolidity. This impression is created by a soft, warm, living chiaroscuro. The sitter must have been pleased with the picture, for Rembrandt, with his unfailing brilliance, created an image depicting the handsome young dandy exactly as he would have wished to see himself. Pictures of this kind helped to establish Rembrandt's popularity with the citizens of Amsterdam.

Meanwhile Rembrandt also continued painting single-figure "history" pictures where models, attired in exotic finery, played the role of some legendary personage, as, for instance, in his *Saskia as Flora* (1634, Hermitage). Here his wife, Saskia van Uylenburgh, appears against a background filled with a mysterious dimness. The cluster of flowers at the right and the flowery staff she holds do not encroach upon the space, serving, rather, to accentuate its depth. Saskia's face and hands, the brilliant colors of the flowers, the solid silk of her mantle, and the gossamer fabric of the sleeves are rendered in a most delicate manner. Saskia is seen as the personification of the mythical goddess of spring and flowers. Indeed, with her own natural beauty, she did not need any idealization to pose as the goddess.

While portraits were numerous enough, "histories" remained Rembrandt's favorites, and it is here that his experiments were particularly varied.

In the early days of his life in Amsterdam Rembrandt did a small grisaille painting known as *The Adoration of the Magi* (1632, Hermitage). Few pictures of that kind survived, but they give us some idea of the early period of his work. Thus, it seems he began to paint limiting his range of colors to white lead, ocher and lamp black, and covering a white ground with broad strokes of dark, slightly translucent brown.

Christ Driving the Money-changers from the Temple. 1626
Oil on panel. 43 × 33 cm (17 × 13")
The Pushkin Museum of Fine Arts, Moscow

The result was a grisaille priming in the beginning, while all the brilliance of the color scheme became apparent only when the painting was completed. Leaving his brownish shadows practically intact, Rembrandt highlighted parts of his figures with whiting, delineating their contours with bold strokes of brown and black. This is the method used in *The Adoration*, though here and there the shape of objects or the texture of their surface is worked out more minutely. X-ray examination has proved that Rembrandt had made many changes as he worked, that he had not been able to achieve at once the composition he had in mind. The canvas had been thought to be a work of Rembrandt's school until it was proved by I. Linnik of the Hermitage in 1968 to have been painted by the master himself.

In composition, *The Incredulity of St. Thomas* (1634, Pushkin Museum) is as typical of some of Rembrandt's narrative pictures as *Portrait of a Young Man* is of his commissioned portraits of the same period; it is reminiscent of a *mise en scène*. In the center, on an elevation, Christ stands risen; the radiance He emanates bathes the figures around Him in light. Such dramatic light effects are quite characteristic of Rembrandt's paintings belonging to that period. The reactions of Christ's disciples and friends to His miraculous appearance before them show various shades of surprise and curiosity — emotions always favored by Rembrandt. The figures of the man in an attitude of prayer, with averted face, and of the sleeper are not so familiar. The picture was certain to meet with approval, for it told a story and served to admonish, while its expressive color scheme charmed the eye.

Another painting belonging to the same period is *The Descent from the Cross* (1634, Hermitage). This canvas continues an iconographic tradition long since established in European art, the highest achievement of which was considered to be Rubens's altarpiece in the Antwerp cathedral, widely known through its engraved reproduction. A comparison with that masterpiece shows Rembrandt's originality. While Rubens depicted venerable and virtuous men and women in sublime grief over a venerable and virtuous hero, Rembrandt paints a scene of distress in the dark of night. Some of the figures have been caught in the light of a lamp, the others remain in darkness, and the impression conveyed is that of a crowd in motion, grieving for the dead and commiserating with the mother. There is nothing spiritual in their appearance, many are coarse and ugly. Like them, Christ is a mere human being; it is in the intensity of their grief that His suffering and death acquire a special meaning. The keynote here is possibly struck by the man who bears the weight of the body, pressing his cheek against it.

Pictures such as *The Descent from the Cross* reveal with exceptional clarity Rembrandt's conception of Biblical themes. Humanist thinkers of the sixteenth and seventeenth centuries, having supplied historical and philological commentaries to the text of the Scriptures, offered a basically new approach to the Bible. The literal interpretation of the Scriptures as a historical source invalidated the centuries-old tradition of allegorical versions that had brought the ancient legend into conformity with the dogma of the Church.

In seventeenth century Holland the triumphant Protestant Church prohibited praying to effigies and drew a line between art and religious worship. A picture on a religious theme now shows a concrete happening, rather than a solemn sacrament, as before. This new approach often forms the basis of an illustrative, prosaic treatment of religious themes in Dutch painting. For Rembrandt it opened entirely new possibilities. Endowed with an extraordinary power of imagination, he could transform the terse phraseology of an ancient text into a scene abounding with detail and tense drama. He endeavored to convey the truth of life as he saw it. In his *Descent from the Cross* Christ the Savior becomes a dead body, giving the theological sense of the action a human meaning. Following the true-to-life principle, Rembrandt, none the less, persistently engaged in extravagant whimsies

Portrait of a Scholar. 1631
Oil on canvas (relined). 104 × 92 cm (41 × 36¹/₄″)
The Hermitage, Leningrad

that are to be found in all his works: from his characteristic chiaroscuro composition of a picture as a whole, all the way to the fantastic details of the Oriental garb of one of the personages.

Thanks to this novel interpretation of the Scriptures, painters now discovered a range of subjects that had not drawn attention before. Taking up the story narrated in the Bible, Rembrandt depicted in his *Parable of the Laborers in the Vineyard* (1637, Hermitage) its closing episode — the owner paying off his laborers. The modest canvas is painted in a free and easy manner. The interior resembles a Dutch merchant's office, portrayed by Rembrandt in accordance with his conception of the picturesque; hence the treatment of the interior space, with its dark, mysterious corners, its arches and vaults, and the alternation of light and shadow on the walls. The stack of ledgers, the bales of goods carelessly piled, the sumptuous tablecloth, the shabby wall, and the birdcage join to create an atmosphere of unkempt domesticity. True-to-life and bizarre elements also mingle in the treatment of the cluster of men, with their vigorous gestures and an exotic note in their attire.

Rembrandt's interpretation of the Biblical story, presented as a real and emotion-filled episode, may almost make the beholder forget the religious meaning of the parable. (The scene of the quarrel between the owner and the laborers is believed by some art historians to be a reflection of social relations in

Holland and, specifically, of the unrest among the apprentices of the Drapers' Guild in Leiden.)

Rembrandt's thinking is remarkable for its down-to-earth propensities, which may be seen in some genre paintings, such as *Parable of the Laborers in the Vineyard*, and even in compositions on the most fantastic subjects. A good example is his *Abraham's Sacrifice* (1635, Hermitage), one of the largest canvases done by him in the 1630s, in which an angel stays Abraham's hand when he is on the verge of sacrificing his son to God. Abraham, caught off guard, drops his knife, showing that only a fleeting instant is recorded by the painter, yet an instant marking the culmination of an act, a moment of great mental tension. Overcome with grief, Abraham can hardly credit his deliverance from the necessity of fulfilling his cruel duty, a deliverance too sudden for him to comprehend and rejoice. Here Rembrandt's experiments in depicting emotion or a passing mood achieve a consummate expressiveness that may be called classical. Particularly apt here would be his own statement, made in one of his letters, that in his art he had endeavored to make "motion as convincing and lifelike as possible."

Depiction of the highest point of physical and mental tension was one of the main objectives of Baroque painting. Rembrandt has much in common with

Portrait of an Old Man. ca. 1643
Oil on panel. 51 × 42 cm (20¹/₈ × 16⁵/₈″)
The Hermitage, Leningrad

6

this style in art, though there is a cardinal difference in its interpretation, despite the general similarity of the problems involved. Rembrandt's true-to-life principle bespeaks a strong bond with national tradition. On the other hand, his "history" pictures consistently challenge the flood of Dutch genre painting, insisting on a different level and different range of artistic conceptions. In the 1630s his work took shape as a truly unique phenomenon in Dutch art of the period, as well as that of Europe in general. The effect of his precepts is markedly evident in his *Danaë* (1636—1646/47, Hermitage). In line with the tradition in European art, the nude figure becomes here the exponent of Rembrandt's aesthetic program, his ideals, aspirations and capabilities.

X-ray examination has shown that the central part of the picture had been painted twice, in two different manners and, consequently, at different times. The barely legible date of 1636 refers to the first variant, whereas the second, final variant was painted probably ten years later. During those ten years Rembrandt's art underwent radical changes that affected not only his thinking, range of interests and self-imposed tasks, but his techniques as well. It was hard for him to go back to a work finished so long ago, to harmonize the old with the new, yet he succeeded in doing just that. He removed certain details, but retained the whimsical splendor of the whole piece. He breathed new life into his heroine: an arm outstretched in a delightful gesture appeared, enticing and warding off at the same time; and the enigmatic play of strong emotions on her face — truly inspired painting that renders the body's life with a force and expressiveness not to be matched. Danaë, the mythical princess awaiting Zeus, her lover, appears here as a woman in a state of great agitation, whose features are far from the classical canon. In this final variant Danaë's image exhibits a more defined emotional and physical state.

Rembrandt's work on *Danaë* shows that his style, while changing from decade to decade, acquired greater continuity and embraced, within each decade, a greater diversity of techniques than is usually thought.

David's Farewell to Jonathan (1642, Hermitage), while belonging to the early 1640s, already reveals the painter's endeavor, characteristic of later years, to reconcile intense mental anguish with outward restraint and concentration. The tearful grief of the youth and Jonathan's stern appearance are alleviated by the remarkable beauty of the color scheme. Splashes of very light and gentle colors on the attire of the two men stand out from the encircling green-tinged haze that fades in the distance, revealing the magnificent architecture of Jerusalem rising beneath a swirl of clouds shot through with mysterious gleams of light. *David's Farewell* is one of the peaks in Rembrandt's development of his favorite theme of a poetical world apart,

The Old Warrior. ca. 1629—30
Oil on panel. 36 × 26 cm (14¹/₄ × 10¹/₄″)
The Hermitage, Leningrad

Portrait of a Boy. 1633
Oil on panel. 67 × 47.5 cm (26³/₈ × 18³/₄″)
The Hermitage, Leningrad

where men and nature are endowed with exalted spiritual essence and beauty.

In the early 1640s Rembrandt began to develop an interest in "genre," or scenes from daily life. This new interest is best revealed in his *Holy Family with Angels* (1645, Hermitage). This canvas is often considered to be a frank depiction of rural life in Holland: Goethe wrote that "Rembrandt had painted Mary using a Dutch peasant girl for a model." The painter's interpretation of the Bible did, in fact, produce realistic scenes with democratic undertones. If we disregard the flock of fluttering cherubs, the *Holy Family* will resemble a genre scene, though the essence of the picture will be human relationships and not a portrayal of daily existence, as in the works of the Dutch genre painters. The central figure, which is the key to the picture's meaning, is Mary, the youthful mother with her love for the Child and her simple cares. These natural human feelings and attachments are depicted here with rare force and beauty. Descending from on high to enter a Dutch carpenter's humble dwelling, the Virgin acquires a new spiritual beauty. On the other hand, ordinary human feelings speak — for the first time in European art — with such an elo-

quent appeal. In this world of simple folk the painter discovers higher values, both human and divine, than are contained in the Biblical story.

During the 1640s the number of portraits painted by Rembrandt fell off considerably, even while they may have acquired greater diversity. His work came to comprise both portraits of romantically costumed personages and pictures intentionally plain in the Dutch tradition. A specimen of the latter is his *Portrait of Baertjen Martens Doomer* (*ca.* 1640, Hermitage); a companion portrait of her husband, Herman Doomer, Rembrandt's frame-maker, dated 1640, is at the Metropolitan Museum in New York. Baertjen is not a society woman: she is the wife of an artisan of modest means connected with the artistic milieu, so that Rembrandt, working on her portrait, was free to follow his artistic inclinations. A master of painting techniques, he knew how to render the finest shades of facial expression. He found something worthy of respect in Baertjen Martens, an energetic woman with a ready tongue, and did his best to show her as she really was.

During the late 1640s a certain convergence becomes noticeable in Rembrandt's commissioned and

The Incredulity of St. Thomas. 1634
Oil on panel. 50 × 51 cm (19³/₄ × 20¹/₈″)
The Pushkin Museum of Fine Arts, Moscow

non-commissioned portraits. In the commissioned portraits he conceives his images more and more on the basis of purely human individual characteristics, as opposed to societal ones, while his non-commissioned portraits increasingly emphasize simplicity and modesty. This trend produced works in which the characteristic features of the former and the latter mingled. Thus, in his *Portrait of an Old Woman* (*ca.* 1650, Pushkin Museum) the voluminous red kerchief, then no longer a customary article of wear (though well liked by Rembrandt), and the old-fashioned Burgundy dress seem to justify the tentative conclusion that the portrait belongs to the non-commissioned series. On the other hand, the strictly subjective treatment of the image seems to class the portrait with the commissioned portraits of earlier years.

In *Portrait of an Old Man* (ca. 1643, Hermitage), on the contrary, the sitter's personality reveals itself through the depiction of his mood: his far from handsome face with its washy features reveals a passive, hopeless acceptance of life's hardships. Here Rembrandt's treatment is more subjective than in *Baertjen Martens* or *Portrait of an Old Woman* or other similar pictures and is akin to the emotional rendering of the personages in his narrative compositions.

The basic problem in Rembrandt's art may be said to be man and his mood, or state of mind. It dominated his life to the last and can be traced, in one form or another, in all of his works, most tangibly in those of the 1650s and 1660s — the period of Rembrandt's highest achievements.

During the 1650s portraiture came to play a particularly important role in Rembrandt's work. A number of outstanding portraits belonging to that period are to be found in Soviet museums. Five canvases (two in Moscow and three in Leningrad) compose what may be regarded as an entirely separate group, comprising non-commissioned portraits of old people, produced around 1654. It is interesting to see how a problem common to all five was solved by the painter in different ways.

The earliest of these was probably the most imposing — *Portrait of an Old Man in Red* (ca. 1652—54, Hermitage). An instance of rare generalization, the portrait renders, none the less, the sitter's individual traits. His motionless pose is nearly symmetrical, with only trifling deviations noticeable in the face and hands and most of all in his gaze, which is slightly turned to the left, toward the source of light, as if the old man, uneasy in the presence of others, did not wish to face them.

The image of a man "alone with himself" occurs in many of Rembrandt's later works. In a state of profound meditation and concentration a man's inner life is revealed in all its complexity and fullness. Showing but a fleeting moment of the stream of life, as art is called upon to do, Rembrandt does it without halting the stream. We can almost read the flux of thoughts and feelings in the old man's face. The portrait inspires a sense of the sitter's unique spiritual life, never the same in the portraits of later years. One cannot help recalling Shakespeare's words: "Time travels in divers paces with divers persons."

Rembrandt's growing comprehension of human character, his ever more profound insight into the dialectics of man's inner life not only determined the composition of all his pictures at that time, but also made him go back again and again to work on the portraits of the selfsame persons. We know, for instance, of one more portrait (*Old Man in an Armchair*, 1652, National Gallery, London) of the same man who had posed for *Old Man in Red*. There exist four likenesses

of a middle-aged man who is considered by some to be Rembrandt's elder brother, Adriaen van Rijn (these portraits are to be found in the museums of Berlin, Paris, the Hague and Moscow). The Moscow picture, dated 1654, shows a man plunged in quiet meditation mixed with despondency. The faint shadow clouding the man's face creates a peculiar atmosphere, both physical and spiritual. Simple at first glance, the Moscow *Portrait of Adriaen van Rijn* conceals many vague, unexpressed possibilities, giving no more than a hint of its rare spiritual wealth.

The models of the other three portraits of 1654, on the contrary, "speak" eloquently about themselves. *Portrait of an Old Woman* and *Portrait of an Old Jew* in the Hermitage are evidently companion pieces. They supplement each other by contrast rather than by similarity.

Portrait of an Old Jew is striking in its dramatic tenseness. His pose, slouched forward and watchful, determines the painter's handling of masses and patches of light that organize the composition. Light accentuates the massive, heavily outlined features. The face reveals in a straightforward manner his mood of bitterness and resentment, and a readiness to put up a fight against anyone, even fate, if need be. Strong emotions grip the old man, forming the substance of his inner world. Both the model and its treatment by the painter are different from *Old Man in Red*, where emotions have ceded to reflection, resulting in a specific attitude toward life that one would wish to call philosophical.

In *Portrait of an Old Woman* (1654, Hermitage) emotions are also plainly apparent. The old woman's head, slightly bowed, and her dejectedly slumped figure must have been observed by the painter in his model. The mood of passive, hopeless resignation to the incredible cruelty of life, dominant in the image, is typical of many Rembrandt's later works.

The same woman sat for *Portrait of an Old Woman* now in Moscow, also dated 1654, which seems to indicate another step in the study of individual character. From rendering a specific mood, no matter how characteristic, the painter passes on to a more profoundly generalized image of man and his fate as a kind of inseparable whole. Refraining from depictions of real-life situations, he portrays "man facing eternity." The Moscow *Portrait of an Old Woman* reveals with remarkable consistency and clarity Rembrandt's credo as a portrait painter.

This type of portrait requires the solution of a number of problems, the most important of which is one's attitude toward life. The individuals depicted in the 1654 series of portraits are marked by a truly tragic philosophy of life; they have learned that there is a great deal of sorrow and cruelty in life, and little justice. They assume that this philosophy is natural and the only one possible, because it is the result of their journey through life, a result reached a long time ago, to which they have become reconciled. Granting the visible isolation of the persons depicted, Rembrandt shows that their rare spirituality lifts them above life's banalities. He imparts to them a touch of supreme nobility and equates their estimation of life with that ultimate truth which expresses a people's world outlook. Rembrandt's "old people" seem to be the personification of human wisdom.

We have been considering works in which the artist apparently tried to give a consummate rendering of his models' personalities. At the same time he continued producing paintings focused more on the emotions or moods of his models than on their characters. A typical example is his *Portrait of a Man* (1661, Hermitage), in which a single mood, that of hopeless despair, shuts out all other thoughts or feelings. In judging this type of work we should keep in mind that for Rembrandt a half-length representation of a model was not necessarily a portrait. His early studies and many later works show that the artist did not intend to give an exhaustive characterization of his models, as is required in portraiture *per se*.

Thus we come to a canvas produced by the master in his declining years: *Portrait of Jeremias De Deck-*

Portrait of an Old Woman. ca. 1650—52
Oil on canvas. 82 × 72 cm (32³/₈ × 28³/₈")
The Pushkin Museum of Fine Arts, Moscow

er, his friend the poet (1666, Hermitage). This time the image shows no overt emotion; here De Decker merely "exists." His vacant gaze reflects an introspective, meditative mood. The portrait belongs to that group of later works in which Rembrandt turned to conventional compositional schemes of the simplest and most neutral kind. In his youth he had shown a keen interest in eloquent gestures, facial expressions and bizarre poses. But now he no longer needed them, for they would have distorted the concept of his picture. In De Decker's portrait the psychological element and the master's style together carry a spiritual message.

The evolution of Rembrandt's "history" painting followed the same lines in the 1650s and 1660s. Compositions with half-figures and no visible action dominated, their protagonists absorbed in their own thoughts and emotions.

Two small "histories" of the 1650s, *Young Woman with Earrings* (1657, Hermitage) and *Christ and the Woman of Samaria* (1659, Hermitage), were followed by three outstanding works executed in the 1660s. In 1660 Rembrandt completed his *Ahasuerus, Haman and Esther* (Hermitage). Taken from the Biblical legend, the central figures, lost in thought, are seated in silence around the table: Ahasuerus, the king of Babylon; Esther, the beautiful Jewess, his wife; and Haman, the king's favorite and an enemy of the He-

Portrait of an Old Woman with Spectacles. 1643
Oil on panel. 61 × 49 cm (24 × 19¹/₄")
The Hermitage, Leningrad

10

brew people. Esther, having just divulged Haman's vicious plans, has lapsed into silence; the king's face reveals the struggle going on in his mind: Haman's life hangs in the balance. These few minutes of suspended action give us a chance to grasp more fully the true worth of each protagonist, their relation to one another, and their fate.

Somewhat later Rembrandt created his *David and Uriah* (1665, Hermitage). Three half-length figures emerge out of a dark background, each exhibiting a strong emotion; this, in the absence of any reference to some definite Biblical episode, offers a possibility of several different interpretations of the subject. The roles of the protagonists are clearly those of an Oriental noble doomed to die and aware of his impending death; a king who is sending him to his death, in sorrow rather than in wrath; and a venerable sage, or prophet perhaps, who grieves as he watches the drama. It has not been determined so far which Biblical episode the painter had in mind: the story of David and Uriah, which is now generally accepted, or the fall of Haman, as previously believed.

In one sense, the magnificent canvas known as *The Return of the Prodigal Son* (ca. 1663, Hermitage) may be considered as the end of a quest that inspired all of Rembrandt's work — the quest of the real, human significance of Biblical stories, the supreme meaning of life. The meeting of the aged father and his son sums up their life on earth, with all the misery they suffered since their parting. The burden of their past weighs heavily upon them and the joy of their reconciliation is tinged with sadness, regret, and repentance.

These three pictures were painted within the same decade. They differ in size, scope, composition and manner, but it is more important to consider that which is common to all three.

The murky darkness flowing around the figures lessens the reality of the scene, but increases the significance of what is taking place, which is reflected in each figure and in the scene as a whole. In Rembrandt's works of the 1630s this was conveyed to some extent by an unusually bizarre and sumptuous setting. In those of the 1640s, such as *The Holy Family*, the dignity of human feeling was conveyed by scenes of daily life. In the "histories" of later years the inner life of the protagonists becomes so intense and meaningful, stirring the painter's compassion to such an extent that there is no longer any room left in the picture for other elements. It is as if the lives of the protagonists are purged of all that could be described as mechanical or accidental. The affinities between the scene depicted and daily life disappear not because of the bizarre surroundings, but because the stream of life flows here on a different and higher spiritual level. In this sense, it may be said that these later works demonstrate the fullest development of the principles

Portrait of an Old Woman. 1654
Oil on canvas (relined). 109 × 84.5 cm (43 × 33¹/₄″)
The Hermitage, Leningrad

that form the base of Rembrandt's "histories" and signal the end of experimentations that determined the course of his artistic career.

The concept of space in Rembrandt's later works has been called "emotionalized space." It would be equally proper to discern the presence of "emotionalized time" in his works. Thus, time stands still for the prodigal son and his father when the tide of emotion engulfs them and all their past life becomes focused in that one minute; while for the silent, motionless witnesses of the reunion the same time pursues a serene, leisurely flow. Time has stopped, run out for Uriah; he is still alive, but might as well be dead. The rhythm of emotion displayed is the rhythm of life itself — the march of destiny for almost all the personages of Rembrandt's paintings.

In the art of Rembrandt's later period human life is closely linked with his concept of fate as something inseparable from a human being while existing outside and above him. One may accept it with good grace or challenge it in spirit, like some of the men whose portraits Rembrandt painted in the 1650s, but there is no use in fighting against it. Seventeenth-century Dutch culture accepted the idea of an ultimate law which no one could evade — be it Calvin's doctrine of predestination or Spinoza's conception of the law of human nature which must be comprehended and accepted as

11

Portrait of Adriaen van Rijn. 1654
Oil on canvas (relined). 74 × 63 cm (29¹/₈ × 24⁷/₈″)
The Pushkin Museum of Fine Arts, Moscow

a guide in life. Rembrandt accepted neither of the two, yet his concept of fate embraced both the idea of God's will and the vast artistic experience of analyzing human psychology, accumulated over the centuries. This might be described as the "inner law," the mold of the individual's character in association with the insurmountable law of life in general.

From the very outset of his career Rembrandt endeavored to see the protagonists of his "histories" as living men and women and succeeded in making them appear as concrete individuals. Among Rembrandt's paintings in Soviet museums, *Danaë* is the most striking example. The system of generalization that is dominant in the artist's works of the 1660s, however, did not call for concreteness: rejecting all secondary or accidental features, he concentrated on the "inner law."

The works of Rembrandt's declining years suggest neither action nor physical activity: the main action has yet to take place (*Ahasuerus, Haman and Esther*) or has just occurred (*David and Uriah, The Return of the Prodigal Son*). The emotional state of the characters does not correlate with the incident and its ramifications; it mirrors the man and the fate that overtakes him. The situation presented in the picture, though intensely dramatic, is important only in so far as it presents a fraction of a continuous flow of time.

Such an interpretation of Biblical legends has little in common with the somewhat illustrative approach

seen in Rembrandt's earlier "histories," for he has deliberately altered the nature and meaning of the episodes recounted in the Scriptures. At Esther's banquet, a scene of struggle and triumph has turned into a scene of passive contemplation. The joyous return of the prodigal son, an allegory of the ultimate reconciliation of the sinner with God, evokes varied emotions — chiefly sadness. In *David and Uriah* there is no direct link with the Biblical story: it is actually a new and different narrative. Its relation to the Bible is more or less the same as that of Shakespeare's tragedy to the medieval chronicle of Hamlet, Prince of Denmark. Using the Bible as a basis, Rembrandt invents his own subjects for his pictures, writes his own tragedies on the themes of the prodigal son, Esther and Haman, and the end of Uriah.

The subjects of Rembrandt's later period are characterized by a definite tragic coloring. That, of course, is explained by the aging painter's distinctive spiritual mold, his attitude towards life in general. His portraits of the 1650s show this attitude to be deeply tragical; and this is abundantly confirmed by his "histories" of the 1660s. His personal misfortunes and the depressing awareness of his isolation in the field of art, which can be traced in some of his self-portraits, must have seriously affected Rembrandt, since the subjective, emotional element had always

Portrait of a Man. 1661
Oil on canvas (relined). 71 × 61 cm (28 × 24″)
The Hermitage, Leningrad

12

Christ and the Woman of Samaria. 1659
Oil on canvas (relined). 60 × 75 cm (23⁵/₈ × 29¹/₅″)
The Hermitage, Leningrad

been of tremendous importance in his work. In addition, the social history of Holland and certain changes in the spiritual climate which manifested themselves in Dutch artistic culture of the mid-seventeenth century had deeply influenced his art, although his personages and their fates show no direct affinity with Dutch social realities.

In his pictures Rembrandt achieved magnificent generalizations. After three centuries they still have the ring of incontestable truth. His personality, conceptions and emotions are visibly present in his works.

It is said that a picture reveals its author's character and, in a sense, serves as his self-portrait. For Rembrandt, this is certainly true.

It goes without saying that a good knowledge of history helps in understanding a great deal of Rembrandt's work. However, it is still more important that we should be capable of direct perception and sympathetic reaction when viewing his works. That Rembrandt's art can still — after a lapse of three centuries — directly affect our inner life is a pledge that it will continue to live.

Xenia Yegorova

BIOGRAPHICAL OUTLINE

1606 Rembrandt Harmensz van Rijn born on July 15, in Leiden, the son of Harmen Gerritsz van Rijn, miller

ca. 1613—20 Studies at the Latin School in Leiden

1620 On May 20 enrolled at Leiden University

ca. 1621—24 Apprenticeship with Jacob Isaaksz van Swanenburgh in Leiden

ca. 1624—25 Six months' association with Pieter Lastman in Amsterdam

ca. 1625 Establishes his own workshop in Leiden

1630 Death of Rembrandt's father, buried in Leiden on April 27

1631 Rembrandt settles in Amsterdam in the house of the art dealer Hendrick van Uylenburgh

1632 *The Anatomy Lesson of Doctor Tulp*

1634 Marriage to Saskia van Uylenburgh, on July 10

1639 Buys a house in Breestraat, where he assembles a large art collection

1641 Birth of his son Titus

1642 June 14: death of Saskia. Rembrandt finishes *The Night Watch*, his greatest canvas

1649 Hendrickje Stoffels enters Rembrandt's household

1654 Birth of Cornelia, daughter of Rembrandt and Hendrickje

1656 Inventory of Rembrandt's possessions made on the occasion of his bankruptcy

1657 Auction sale of his collections

1658 Sale of Rembrandt's house. The family moves to Rosengracht, where Hendrickje and Titus set up as art dealers

1661—62 Rembrandt finishes his monumental *Conspiracy of Claudius Civilis*

1662 Finishes his group portrait of *The Sampling Officials of the Drapers' Guild*

1663 Death of Hendrickje Stoffels, buried in Amsterdam on July 24

1668 Death of Titus, buried in Amsterdam on September 7

1669 Death of Rembrandt on October 4; buried in the Westerkerk, Amsterdam, on October 8

PLATES

THE ADORATION OF THE MAGI. 1632
Oil on paper pasted on canvas. 45 × 39 cm (17³/₄ × 15³/₈″). Grisaille
The Hermitage, Leningrad

PORTRAIT OF A YOUNG MAN WITH A LACE COLLAR. 1634
Oil on panel. 70×52 cm ($27^5/_8 \times 20^1/_2''$, oval)
The Hermitage, Leningrad

SASKIA AS FLORA. 1634

Oil on canvas (relined). 125 × 101 cm (49$^{1}/_{4}$ × 39$^{3}/_{4}$")
The Hermitage, Leningrad

THE DESCENT FROM THE CROSS. 1634
Oil on canvas (relined). 158 × 117 cm (62¹/₄ × 46″)
The Hermitage, Leningrad

ABRAHAM'S SACRIFICE. 1635
Oil on canvas (transferred from the old one).
193 × 132.5 cm (76 × 52$^1/_8$")
The Hermitage, Leningrad

PARABLE OF THE LABORERS IN THE VINEYARD. 1637
Oil on panel. 31×42 cm ($12^1/_4 \times 16^1/_2''$)
The Hermitage, Leningrad

PORTRAIT OF BAERTJEN MARTENS DOOMER. *ca.* 1640
Oil on panel. 76 × 56 cm (30 × 22")
The Hermitage, Leningrad

DAVID'S FAREWELL TO JONATHAN. 1642
Oil on panel. 73 × 61.5 cm (28³/₄ × 24¹/₄″)
The Hermitage, Leningrad

THE HOLY FAMILY. 1645
Oil on canvas (relined). 117×91 cm ($46 \times 35^7/_8''$)
The Hermitage, Leningrad

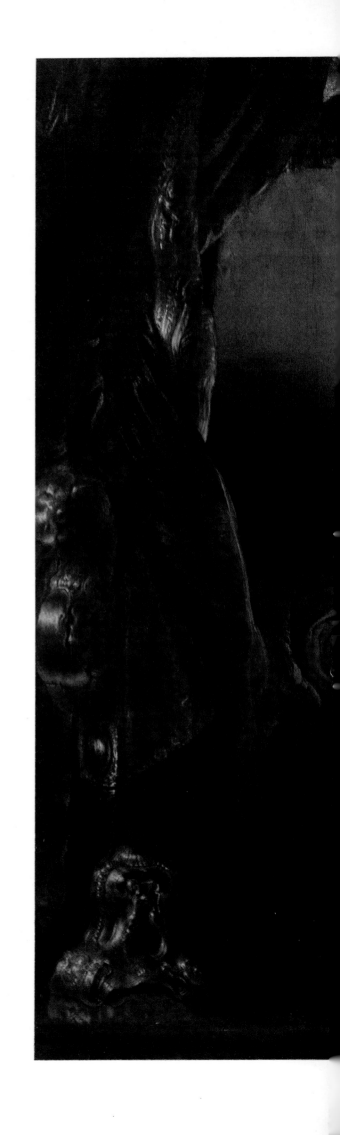

DANAË. 1636—1646/47
Oil on canvas (relined). 185 × 203 cm (72⁷/₈ × 80″)
The Hermitage, Leningrad

PORTRAIT OF AN OLD MAN IN RED. *ca.* 1652—54
Oil on canvas (relined). 108×86 cm ($42^1/_2 \times 33^7/_8''$)
The Hermitage, Leningrad

PORTRAIT OF AN OLD JEW. 1654
Oil on canvas (relined). 109 × 84.8 cm (45 × 33³/₈″)
The Hermitage, Leningrad

PORTRAIT OF AN OLD WOMAN. 1654

Oil on canvas (relined). 74 × 63 cm (29^1/$_8$ × 24^7/$_8$″)
The Pushkin Museum of Fine Arts, Moscow

YOUNG WOMAN WITH EARRINGS. 1657
Oil on panel. 39.5 × 32.5 cm (15$^1/_2$ × 12$^3/_4$″)
The Hermitage, Leningrad

THE RETURN OF THE PRODIGAL SON. *ca.* 1663
Oil on canvas (relined). 262 × 205 cm (103$\frac{1}{8}$ × 80$\frac{3}{4}$″)
The Hermitage, Leningrad

AHASUERUS, HAMAN AND ESTHER. 1660
Oil on canvas (relined). 73 × 94 cm (28³/₄ × 37″)
The Pushkin Museum of Fine Arts, Moscow